Ignatius J

P's & Q's AND WORDS OF

INSPIRATION

VOL 2

"The best use of life is to spend it for something that outlast it."

-William James

Frankie Delores James

February 6, 1952- January 26, 1976

Young Ms. Frankie

The first funeral I attended was February 7, 1976, I was five years old. My cousin Frankie was shot and killed by three white men, James M. Thornton Jr. (30), Kendrick, Clay Cain (18) and Charles Rasco (26) eight days before her 23rd birthday. Her funeral was the day after what would have been her 23rd birthday. One weird thing that I discovered about the death of my cousin, Frankie James, is two of the names of the killers was James and Charles. One of her younger brothers' names is Charles James. I was told that her brother Charles was an apprentice of her boyfriend, the drug dealer. Cousin Frankie was my aunt Dot's second daughter to pass away. My mother and Frankie were the same age and were the best of friends even though they were aunt and niece. Frankie was four days older than my mother. From my understanding my 22-year-old cousin Frankie's murder was a set up. Her boyfriend at the time was a big-time drug dealer in Memphis, Tennessee. The three white men that entered her and her roommate Mary Jones's apartment that fatal night claimed to be narcotics officers.

Memphis, Tennessee newspaper report reads:
"January 30, 1976

$25,000 Bonds Set for 3 in Woman's Death

Miss James (Frankie) was forced at gunpoint to lie on the floor with her roommate, Mary Brown, as the men attempted to handcuff them, police said. Police said Miss Brown was handcuffed on both wrists and that Miss James had one wrist handcuffed when the shot was fired. The bullet struck her in the left arm and then went into her body through the back, fatally wounding her. The slaying was reported to police shortly after the men left. Miss Brown telephoned police. She said the shooting took place at 11:40 p. m. Miss James was pronounced dead at City of Memphis Hospital at 12:50 a. m. yesterday. George Hutchinson, deputy chief for operations, said police "definitely were not involved in this matter. Those men were posing as narcotics officers but they have no connection with our Metro Narcotics Squad. Lt William Schultz said they knocked on the door, identified themselves as "narcotics officers, and were admitted." He said they then "asked where the heroin was" and told the women to lie down. He said when the shot was fired the men grabbed a small gray fire safe with a combination lock and fled. The safe had not been recovered last night. The handcuffs, a Smith & Wesson brand, are available at a number of surplus stores, Hutchinson said. Police said they found two marijuana cigarettes and a small quantity of loose marijuana in the apartment. A neighbor said the women "lived a real strange life -style. There were so many cars coming and going in and out. Other neighbors said it was not unusual to hear knocking on the apartment door at any hour of the day or night. But Sue Duncan, resident manager of the English Village Apartments where the slaying took place, said the women "were real good tenants. I had received no complaints on them". She said the $198 monthly rental was always paid on time by a woman known as Mrs. Parks".

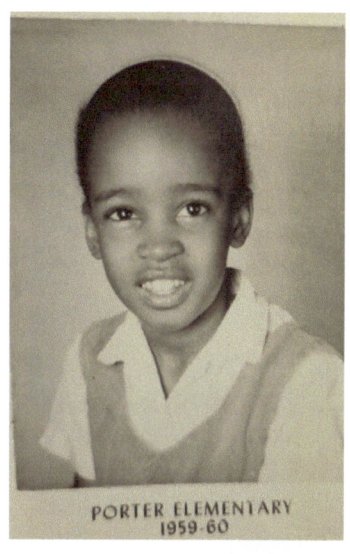

PORTER ELEMENTARY
1959-60

Regardless of their reasons it was undoubtedly a horrific act that shook my family and changed the course of her only child, her six-year-old son Chris's life forever! I was too young to understand what was going on, but I understood that my cousin Frankie was gone forever, and that sadness and mourning was among my family.

Table of Contents

Acknowledgments

My CREATOR, the universe, my ancestors –I am thankful for being able mentally, physically, spiritually, and emotionally. I am grateful for those that love me and those that I love. I am grateful for Wednesday and Winter. I am appreciative for the material things that I have been allowed to have along my journey. May my ancestors continue to protect, guide, and uplift me as I walk the paths that the universe has laid before me that my HIGER POWER created for me to follow.

Frankie Delores James

Death leaves a heartache no one can heal, love leaves
a memory no one can steal.

Unknown

Living Life

Nobody wants to be around someone who's always
got something negative to say.
Don't come messing with my peace just because
you can't find yours
Unknown

Note to self:
*Goal without Deadline = Fantasy
*Goal + Deadline = Objective
*Goal + Deadline + Plan = Intention
*Goal + Deadline + Plan + Consistent Action = Success
*Personal Meaningful Goal + Deadline + Plan + Consistent Action =
Fulfillment
Unknown

"Money is the root to all evil"
I've heard and read that all my
life. The root is "YOU".
Ignatius J 13JAN2018

"Choose your leaders with wisdom and forethought.
To be led by a coward is to be controlled by all that
the coward fears.
To be led by a fool is to be led by the opportunists who control the fool.
To be led by a thief is to offer up your most precious
treasures to be stolen.
To be led by a liar is to ask to be told lies.
To be led by a tyrant is to sell yourself and those you love into slavery."
Octavia E. Butler, Parable of the Talents

May you attract someone who speaks your language so
you don't have to spend a lifetime translating your soul
Unknown

"You can forgive some people without
welcoming them back into your life.
Apology accepted; access denied."
Freetheinfo.com

Go Again!
Apply Again!
Try Again!
YOUR Again is
about to be A GAIN!
Unknown

"Dreams
Hold fast to dreams
For if dreams die
Life is a broken-winged
bird That cannot fly.
Hold fast to dreams
For when dreams go
Life is a barren field
Frozen with snow."
Langston Huges

You are not important because of how long you live,
you are important because of how effective you live . . .
Unknown

THE 3 RULES OF I'M SORRY

1. The first sorry can be excused.
2. The second sorry means that you're aware, but you're still falling into old habits.
3. The third sorry means you don't care and I'mma have to fuck you up.

Unknown

3 RULES IN LIFE

1. If you don't go after what you want. You'll never get it.
2. And if you do not ask, the answer will always be no.
3. If you do not step forward, you will remain in the same place.

Unknown

When someone ghost you,
respect the dead and
move on
Unknown

"Some people are so heavenly minded
that they are no earthly good"
Oliver Wendall Holmes

THE ART OF LIFE
LIES IN A
CONSTANT
READJUSTMENT
TO OUR
SURROUNDINGS
Okakura Kakuzo

Be so completely yourself that
everyone else feels safe to be
themselves too
Unknown

STOP thinking you have
more of me than you do.
-Time
Unknown

"Normal is an illusion.
What's normal for the spider
is chaos for the fly."
Morticia Addams – The Addams Family

"People come and they go ... They tell you they love you today and throw you away tomorrow. Society is infested with SOULESS, NARCISSIST, BROKEN, MESSED UP TOXIC PEOPLE. However, the key is to give these types of people no access into your life and to learn how to stop, vet them and keep them out of your inner temple and maintain your sanity, safety and sanctuary of peace. It's important to be able to let them go on their way, without getting upset or be left feeling used or abused. Be guided by Ancestors your spirit guides and most of all your higher self and listen to your emotions and feelings, but not be controlled by them and let your freedom of choice and behavior never weigh you down like an anchor"

www.freetheinfo.com

"When's the last time you heard someone say, "Remember that time I paid 40k on that car that I traded in for that newer car three years later?" Or how about, "Man, this new 70-inch plasma/Hd/4D/Tv really fulfills my days with happiness!" Or how about, "That 3k I dropped on Christmas morning, even though they only play with/ use 5% of them." Or how about, "We finally paid that mortgage off completely, time to really start living life and planning some trips." Chasing the bag" is all well and good but what all are you missing while you're chasing it? It's a never-ending race if you participate too much. Life is about accumulating memories and experiences, not possessions and material things."

#WWLVD

Photo by Ignatius J

"Be the person who breaks the cycle. If you were judged, choose understanding. If you were rejected, choose acceptance. If you were shamed, choose compassion. Be the person you needed when you were hurting, not the person who hurt you. Vow to be better than what broke you –to heal instead of becoming bitter so you can act from your heart, not your pain."

-Lori Deschene Soul Vibes

"Don't judge the choices of people. Don't criticize the decisions of people; as you don't know the real story behind it. Every person has a story, every situation influences decisions; without knowing about this story. Don't judge any person."

-Harina

Never regret anything that has happened in your life,
it cannot be changed, undone or forgotten so
take it as a lesson learned and move on
Unknown

There are people speaking nicely about you behind your back.
People are conspiring about ways to help you.

People are advocating for you.
People are genuinely rooting for you behind your back.
Not everyone is against you although it may feel like it at times
Unknown

"We have to realize that some people are just not for you
and not meant to run with you in this next season!
You can't love out the RED FLAGS"
Sandra Benaglia Smith

"I survived because the fire inside of me burned
brighter than the fire around me."
Joshua Graham

Cheating is a personal decision.
Some people will never cheat
no matter how hard things are;
others will always cheat no matter
how good they have it
Unknown

From now on, I'm NOT putting up with
any HATERATION or HOLLERATION in my
DANCERY
Ignatius J 07/16/24

Unfortunately, some people were not put here to evolve.
They are here to remind you what it looks like
if you don't
Unknown

I don't need all the money in the world.
I just need enough money to see the world.
Unknown

Forgive them, even if they aren't sorry.
Let them **be right** if that's what
they need. Send them **love** and send them off.
Don't tie yourself to small mindedness.
It will steal your wellbeing.
Unknown

"What fascinates me is that hardly anyone is wondering
what we're actually doing on this planet. Most accepted the work-
entertainment-sleep cycle as life and have no desire for deeper
understanding of our purpose in this universe."
Jim Carrey

When something good happens,
travel to celebrate.
If something bad happens,
travel to forget it.
If nothing happens,
travel to make something happen
Unknown

Laziness kills **ambition**
Anger kills **wisdom**
Fear kills **dreams**
Ego kills **growth**
Jealousy kills **peace**
Doubt kills **confidence**
Now read that right to left
Unknown

"Criticism is worth so
much more than
compliments"
G-Easy

"Sadness is caused by intelligence,
the more you understand certain things,
the more you wish you didn't understand them"
Charles Bukowski

Teachers won't make you smart.
Mentors won't make you rich.
Trainers won't make you fit.
People can help you, but
Growth is your responsibility.
unknown

"People think they're competing
with other suitors when dating me,
but really, I'm comparing you to my
own solitude. That's the competition.
Is your company better than being alone?
Am I growing around you like I do when
I'm alone? Do I feel safe? Is there joy???
Is there peace??"
KAYA NOVA @thekayanova

Don't confuse what God wanted you to go through,
with what you decided to deal with
Zigg @XaviercMiller

"Never wound a snake;
kill it"
Harriet Tubman

"Healing makes you realize some people don't
deserve to be around you, no matter how much
you love them. Unconditional love doesn't mean
unconditional tolerance of abuse, disrespect, or
bull-shit – it's not unconditional boundaries"
Pammy DS – Selflovehealer

"When a bird is alive, it eats ants.
When the bird is dead, ants eat the bird.
Time & circumstances can change at any
time. Don't devalue or hurt anyone in life.
You may be powerful today. But remember,
time is more powerful than you! One tree
makes a million match sticks. Only one match
stick is needed to burn a million trees . . .
So be good and do good."
KARMA

Don't rock the boat unless
you have a plan to get me back
to shore
Unknown

"Yes, they broke your heart. Yes, you did not get that job.
Okay, your visa application was denied. But no matter
your disappointment, refuse to stay down. Cry the first day,
be melancholy the second day. But like your Saviour, you
must rise on the third day. You were betrayed for a reason. It
is part of the plan. Without your Judas, you can't have your
resurrection. See things from God's perspective. You were not
rejected in that relationship. You were protected from that
relationship. If a tree won't yield you fruit, there is no point in
seeking shade under it. Move on. Don't make the pain permanent.
Let your hurt be like the moon. It appears at night and is gone by
morning. Your so-called setback is a setup for a step up and a
comeback!"
King Wisdom

Photo by Ignatius J

Ignorance is deadly. So much poison can be pumped into
an individual's mind, that all they see is "black or white". Sadly,
there are some brother's out there that will kill another brother if he's
wearing red or blue. There are some "white" people that will
kill "black" people because they have "black" skin, light skin, dark
skin, brown skin. "African American", "Black", "Negro", "Nigger",
"Nigga", "Spook", "Goon". American (His-Story) history, please don't
allow "HIS-Story" mess up "YOUR-HISTORY".
Dark skin and light skin and everything in-between. Stevie Wonder can
see that colors are beautiful in every shade because he see's
that beauty is deeper than the color of skin.
Ignatius J 10APR2025

"I don't know how World War III will be fought,
but I do know World War IV will be fought with
sticks and stones."
Albert Einstein

"Religion is what keeps the poor
from murdering the rich"
-Napoleon Bonapart

"Humans invented the atomic
bomb, but no mouse in the
world would construct a
mousetrap"
Albert Einstein

"If money problems are your only problems,
trust me, you're OK.
I've had bad credit THREE times, but I've
NEVER had bad CREDIBILITY.
Just get some more money . . . and do right
by it once you get it.
You're not in REAL trouble til you're having
mental/spiritual/physical/emotional health
issues.
Learn how to say AND I MEAN . . .
FUCK THEM FOLKS . . .
and FUCK THAT SHIT."
Aishia Taylor

"We come from broken homes, the hood,
childhood traumas, and sad stories. We
are not hustling to impress or be in
competition with anyone. We just want
to change the storyline for ourselves and our
kids and win battles our parents never won!"
Miguel Rodriguez

The sun upgrades your DNA
The moon strengthens your psychic
abilities
Trees absorb negative energy
The ocean cleanses your aura
Unknown

If you got to lie to me,
just say bye to me
Ignatius J 20OCT2020

Infancy: birth until the age one; 12 months.

Early childhood/ Toddler: one until three years old.

Preschooler: three until five years old.

Middle childhood/ Grade-schooler: five until twelve years old.

Teen: thirteen until eighteen years old.

(**Adolescence**): twelve until 20 years old.

Young adult: eighteen until 21 years old.

New adult/ emerging adult: 21 until 29.

(**Early adulthood**): 20- 35.

Midlife: 35- 50.

Mature adult: 50- 80.

(**Senior citizen**): 65+

Late adulthood: 80+

12 years a child and 68 years as an adult (Maybe)

40+ hours a week. 20+ years until retirement (Maybe). Life expectancy for men 74.8 for women 80.2 (Maybe). Most people don't retire until 65+ years of age

giving them MAYBE 10 OR 15 years to enjoy, said, retirement.

F#$% the norm and live your BEST LIFE every chance you get,

EVERY DAY!!

Ignatius J 08AUG2022

"How in the hell could a man enjoy being awakened at 6:30 a.m. by an alarm clock, leap out of bed, dress, force-feed, shit, piss, brush teeth and hair, and fight traffic to get to a place where essentially you made lots of money for somebody else and were asked to be grateful for the opportunity to do so?"

-*Charles Bukowski*

9 to 5

"Tumble out of bed and I stumbled to the kitchen
Pour myself a cup of ambition
And yawn and stretch and try to come to life
Jump in the shower and the blood starts pumpin'
Out on the street, the traffic starts jumpin'
With folks like me on the job from nine to five
It's enough to drive you crazy if you let it
Nine to five, for service and devotion
You would think that I would deserve a fair promotion
Want to move ahead but the boss won't let me
I swear sometimes that man is out to get me
They let you dream just to watch 'em shatter
You're just a step on the bossman's ladder
But you've got dreams he'll never take away.
In the same boat with a lot of your friends
Waitin' for the day your ship'll come in.
And the tides gonna turn an' it's all gonna roll your way
Working nine to five, what a way to make a livin'
Barely gettin' by, it's all takin' and no givin'
They just use your mind and you never get the credit
It's enough to drive you crazy if you let it
Nine to five, yeah, they got you where they want you
There's a better life and you think about it don't you
It's a rich man's game no matter what they call it
And you spend your life puttin' money in his wallet"
Dolly Parton

Women are the portals to this earth
from one realm to another. What we
call "spirit world" to material world
(earth)
Unknown

"Stop introducing people to
a version of you that
you can't maintain."
@ mr_monkee

"Years of love have been forgot,
in the hatred of a minute."
Edgar Allan Poe

"There are two types of people:
1. "I'm not going to help that person, because nobody helped me."
2. "I'm going to help that person because I know how it felt when nobody helped me."
The type of person you choose to be will be the type of energy you attract in your life."
#saiitheartist

There are people who will shoot themselves in the foot as long as they're standing on someone else's foot
Unknown

"A wise man told me don't argue with fools.
Cause people from a distance can't tell who
is who."
Jay Z

"Never argue with stupid people, because
they will drag you down to their level and
then beat you with experience."
Mark Twain

"Better to remain silent and
be thought a fool than to
speak and remove all doubt."
Abraham Lincoln

"I'm in that guy's dream.
You have to be wise enough
to know when you're
living in your dream, and be
humble enough to
accept when you're in someone else's!"
Be humble!"
Dave Chappelle

"Men, are valued for a how
many women they can
slay. Women, on the other
hand, are valued by
how pure they can stay."
Sharpe Fit

"No matter what life throws at me, I will never stop loving it. What I make out of it is up to me. Life is tough but so am I. And here's a thing, I'm a nice person. So, if I'm a bitch to you, you need to ask yourself why."
I am Marcus

"Most don't understand the old were once young. No matter their mistakes made, the wisdom of life remains within them."
@real_tcfinesse

Photo by Ignatius J

"Everywhere I go I prosper. Everything I
do always work out for me. I welcome
new energy. I am attracting better. I feel
good about who I am. I love myself. I choose
to be hopeful. I believe in myself. I am thriving
in every way. Things are happening for me now."
*IDIL AHMED * IDILLIONAIRE*

Some people are getting their karma
and they have to stand on what they
did. If they ever want to get out of their
deficit they have to become better people
Unknown

The problem with closed
minded people is their mouth
is always open
unknown

As you get older, you'll realized that a $30,000 watch and a $30 watch both tell the same time.

A Gucci wallet and a target wallet holds the same amount of money.

A $10 million house and a $100,000 house host the same loneliness.

A Ford will also drive you as far as a Bentley.

True happiness is not found in materialistic things, it comes from the love and laughter found with each other.

Stay humble... the holes dug for us in the ground are the same size.

Unknown

"Pleasure in the job puts perfection in the work."

-Aristotle

There's a difference between taking advantage of an opportunity and taking an opportunity for granted. Know the difference and maybe you can live a better life. When you know better, you're supposed to do better.

Ignatius J 09SEP2024

If God Should Go on Strike

"If only once He'd given up and said, "That's it, I'm through! "I've had enough of those on earth, so this is what I'll do. "I'll give my orders to the sun — cut off the heat supply! "And to the moon — give no more light, and run the oceans dry. "Then just to make things really tough and put the pressure on, "Turn off the vital oxygen till every breath is gone!" You know He would be justified, if fairness was the game, for no one has been more abused or met with more disdain than God, and yet He carries on, supplying you and me with all the favors of His grace, and everything for free. Men say they want a better deal, and so on strike they go, but what a deal we've given God to whom all things we owe. We don't care whom we hurt to gain the things we like; But what a mess we'd all be in, if God should go on strike."

Walt Huntley

You So Black

"You so Black, You so Black! When you smile, the stars come out. You so Black, when you're born, the God come out Black as night. Black when it's wrong and Black when it's right Black is pyramids and mathematics Black is melanized magic. Black is televised and in need of drastic Black advancement. Black enhances Black with chances Black with privilege Black with pride Black on purpose on the black hand side Black and beautiful Black and blessed and highly favored, praise the Lord Black and blessed Black and so much more Black and nothing less Black and educated Black is brilliant Black is strong Black is resilient."

Theresa @thasongbird

"How many "AGAINS" are you
going to begin?? How many "
AGAINS " with the same ol
arguments?? How many "AGAINS"
to realize this is NOT heaven sent??
How many "AGAINS " with the
abandonments?? How many "AGAINS"
with the same ol END?? NOTHING will
change if your "AGAIN" is the same."
Ignatius J 31JAN2025

"F-E-A-R
Has two meanings:
'Forget Everything And Run'
'Face Everything And Rise'
The choice is yours."
-Zig Ziglar

A matter of a **FACT** . . .
it's really sad
not realizing that I wanted,
and needed a father in my life
until I got older. Because the
environment I grew up in, I
thought fatherless children
was
"normal".
Ignatius J 14NOV23

"Salary is a tool that pays the rent for
the bed you sleep in, in order to for you
to dream."
Warren Buffett

Loyalty to iniquity

"Loyalty to iniquity, loyalty to dysfunction, loyalty to brokenness, loyalty to bad habits, loyalty to fear, loyalty to poverty, loyalty to trauma, loyalty to idols and images, loyalty to the Pharaohs of our lives, and the list goes on and on. Sadly, it's still running rampant today, eclipsing the hearts and the souls of those brainwashed, whitewashed, social media-washed, red washed, blue washed, lulled into unconsciousness by the constant white noise of self-hatred and self-sabotage -the byproduct of systematic hope deferred via institutionalized injustices where entire communities experience delayed or denied opportunities generation after generation."

Unknown

"Emancipate yourself from mental slavery,
none but ourselves can free our mind."
Once lost, freedom is hard to restore.
-Bob Nester Marley

"You'll always get whatever you want
when you realize you are the one who has
to get up and go get it."
AVERSTU.COM

"You need to get up, get out, and get
something, don't let the days of your life
pass you by. You need to get up, get out
and get something, don't spend all your
time tryna to get high. You need to get up,
get out, and get something, how will you
make it if you don't even try? You need to get
up, get out, and get something 'cause you and
I got to do for you and I."
Outkast

"I was not born into this world to be
a victim, I was born to be a warrior.
When a man sees himself as a victim,
he is no longer a free man. Nobody needs
to put chains on his body, because the
chains are already in his mind."
-Shaka Zulu

"Some of you are unaware of just how amazing you
really are. The way you make people laugh, lift others
up or spread some extra love . . . You do this even though
you are struggling too, and I think it makes you such a
fucking beautiful human being."
Derrick Cox

Don't miss out on your life
trying to get it together
Unknown

Photo by Ignatius J

"A lot of problems can be solved just by removing some food, some people, and some habits from your life."
Matthew McConaughey

Every bite you take is either, fighting disease OR feeding it.
True story. YOUR life depends on it. It's YOUR story.
Unknown

"There's no one to impress.
Live well for you. Improve for
you. Most don't get it."
Unknown

"Sometimes you can play a role in your own suffering by standing by waiting for other people to change instead of being accountable and deciding what you will no longer tolerate.

Remember that you have to be an active participant in creating the change you seek in your life."
Minaa B., LMSW @MinaaBe

If you never get off of the couch, you're guaranteed not to get into trouble . . . but you'll also miss out on everything in life.
Unknown

"The patten has repeated
because the work is
incomplete."
Devi Brown

Grow, so what your parents did or did not do can stop
ruining your life,

your children's life, your spouse's life, your coworker's life, the bus
driver's life, and the life of everyone around you, and connected to
you and love you. Be what they were at their best and share it with the
world. The chaotic dysfunctional mess that they were is not you but
taught you who you do not want to be and who you want to be. Grow.
Ignatius J 02Oct2022

5 Ways NOT to be USED
1. Believe in Patterns NOT Apologies
2. Don't fall in love with Potential
3. Believe all RED FLAGS
4. Know YOUR WORTH!!!
5. Don't lower your STANDARDS!
Unknown

"Humans beings in a mob
What's a mob to a king?
What's a king to a god?
What's a god to a non-believer?
Who don't believe in anything?
Will he make it out alive?
No church in the wild
Tears on the mausoleum floor
Blood stains the Colosseum doors
Lies on the lips of a priest
Thanksgiving disguised as a feast."
Jay Z/ Frank Ocean/ Kanye West

"The fault, dear Brutus is not in our stars,
but in ourselves, that we are the underlings."
Shakespeare

"The evil that men do lives after them;
the good is oft interred with their bones."
Shakespeare

"You gotta resurrect the deep pain within you and give it a place to live that's not within your body.

Let it live in art. Let it live in writing. Let it live in music. Let it be devoured by building brighter connections.

Your body is not a coffin for pain to be buried in. Put it somewhere else."

iya eh –hee –may @ehimeora

"Sometimes, you get what you want.

Other times, you get a lesson in patience, timing, alignment, empathy, compassion, faith, perseverance, humility, trust, meaning, awareness, resistance, purpose, clarity, grief, beauty, and life.

Either way, you win."

-Brianna West

21 days can build a habit, 90 days can build
a new lifestyle. It takes 3 months to change
your life essentially.
It's not easy, but it's simple."

Unknown

Did you know butterflies rest when it rains
cause it damages their wings? It's okay to
rest during the storms of life. You'll always
fly again once it's over.
Unknown

"Most don't understand the old were once
young. No matter their mistakes made, the
wisdom of life remains within them."
@real_tcfinesse

Note to self:
All you have to do is show up. Be late. Be scared.
Be a mess. Be weird. Be confused. Just BE there.
You'll figure out the rest as you go.
Unknown

"We want to find exactly how, when, and where our natural desires have wrapped us. We wish to look squarely at the unhappiness this has caused others and ourselves. By discovering what our emotional deformities are, we can move toward their correction."

Today I am no longer a slave to alcohol, yet so many ways enslavement still threatens -myself, my desires, even my dreams. Yet without dreams I cannot exist; Without dreams there is nothing to keep me moving forward.

I must look inside myself, to free myself. I must call upon God's power to face the person I feared the most, the true me, the person God created me to be. Unless I can or until I do, I will always be running and never be truly free. I ask God daily to show me such a freedom!"

AN INSIDE LOOK/ TWELVE STEPS AND TWELVE TRADITIONS p. 43 APRIL 8

"For just as the body without the spirit is dead, so also, faith without work is dead."

James 2:26

The universe responds to your frequency. It doesn't recognize your personal desires, wants or needs. It only understands the frequency in which you are vibrating at. For example; if you are vibrating in the frequency of fear, guilt or shame you are going to attract things of a similar vibration. If you are vibrating in the frequency of love, joy and abundance, you are going to attract things that support that frequency. It's kinda like tuning into a radio station. You have to be tuning into the music you want to listen to just like you have to be tuned into the energy you want to manifest into your life. Change your mindset, it will change your life.

Unknown

No, I'm NOT going to be who YOU want me to be, NOT entirely. How could I be? Why would I want to be? Be what someone else wants me to be? ENTIRELY? To show loyalty? What about loyalty to myself OR should I put that on a shelf? You want me to be good? Good to who, you? What about being good to myself so that I could share that goodness with you and everyone else OR is that something else I should hide in the back of the shelf? You want me to have love and respect. For whom, you? Love and respect I have, and I'll share it with you freely and show not just you but everyone I come across sympathy and empathy. It's just who I already am. YOU want me to show those traits the way you show them and when I don't it's me you want to condemn. I am NOT YOU, and YOU are NOT me. Thats facts on fact and on that we can agree to disagree, agree, or put it in the back of the shelf and let it be. The way I show love and respect towards others is the way I do, and I do it sincerely and genuinely. It may not be up to your standards and that's okay. You live your life your way, and I'll continue to live my life my way. I'm NOT going to "act" the way YOU want me to act. I am NOT an actor. YOU are NOT my director. So, let's get it straight. In this movie, my life, I am the director and that never was and never will be up for debate. No disrespect or hate. Every step I make; I create. Every breath I take is no mistake. Grateful and thankful for this life that I have been granted to be in charge of and this vessel that I have been allowed to dwell in. Code-switching is NOT my thing. My authenticity is one of my beautiful attributes and what I bring. There is

NOTHING I need OR lack for me to change the way I act. I will NOT therefore

I CAN NOT talk the way YOU want me to talk. Walk the way YOU want me to walk, I WILL NOT. I am NOT you. I am NOT your creation. I am NOT your marionette.

Ignatius J 03MAR25

Friendships

"That's what real love amounts to -

Letting a person be what he really is. Most people love you for who you pretend to be. To keep their love, you must keep pretending -performing. You get to love your pretense. It's true, we're locked in an image, and act -and the sad thing is, people get used to their image, they grow attached to their masks. They love their chains. They forget all about who they really are. And if you try to remind them, they hate you for it, they feel like you're trying to steal their most precious possession."

Dash Jim Morrison

"Friends is a word we use every day

Most the time we use it in the wrong way

Now you can look the word up, again and again

But the dictionary doesn't know the meaning of friends

And if you ask me, you know, I couldn't be much help

Because a friend's somebody you judge for yourself

Some are okay, and treat you real cool

And some mistake your kindness for being a fool

We like to be with some, because they're funny

Others come around when they need some money

Some you grew up with, around the way

And you're still real close to this very day

Homeboys through the summer, winter, spring and fall

And then there's some we wish we never knew at all

And this list goes on, again and again

But these are the people that we call friends"

Whodini

"You want to know who your friends are?
Start your own business and ask for
their support."
Steve Jobs

"My ex's didn't "miss out' on ANYTHING,
we just weren't meant to be. Folks gotta STOP
being weird & acting like they're the
BEST option on earth for someone."
Millionaire @TheRealDrePapi

"They WON'T find someone "better than you".
They WILL find someone better FOR them, than you,
and so will you."
Joel (Jo-el) Leon @JoelakaMaG

"When someone falls in love with
your flowers & not your roots, they
don't know what to do once fall & winter
come."
Jade Jackson @IAMJADEJACKSON

Money gets a man, the woman he wants.
Struggle gets a man, the woman he needs.
When he's NOT struggling anymore and have money
does he not get the woman he wants and needs??
Beauty gets a woman the man she wants.
Struggle gets a woman . . .
Ignatius J 07APR2025

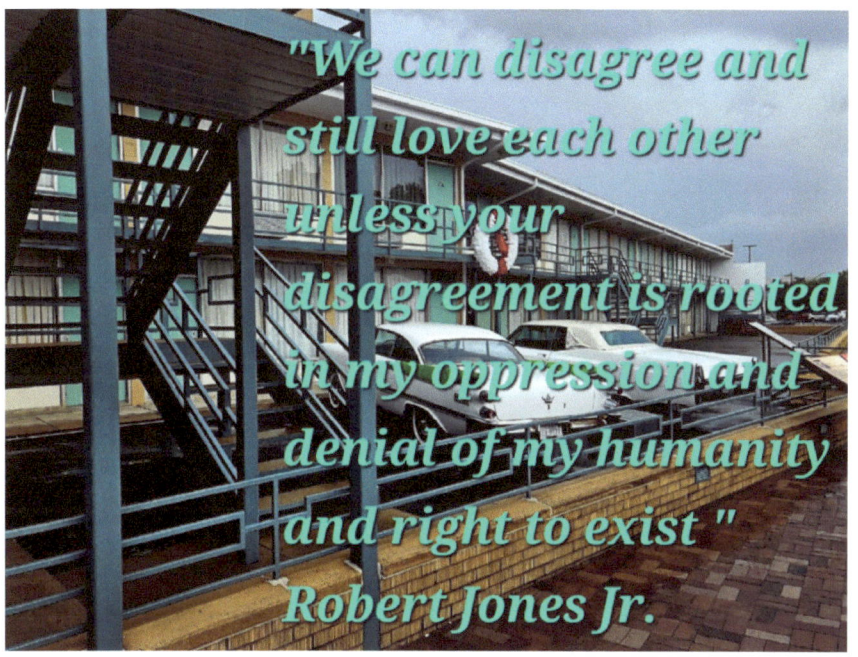

"We can disagree and still love each other unless your disagreement is rooted in my oppression and denial of my humanity and right to exist "
Robert Jones Jr.

Photo by Ignatius J

I was thinking; if we could stop
calling each other negative names
and just call each other brother
but then I remembered: Cain
called Able, brother
Ignatius J 03OCT16

"We can disagree and still
love each other unless your
disagreement is rooted in
my oppression and denial
of my humanity and right
to exist."
Robert Jones Jr.

There's a saying in Germany. If there's a Nazi
at the table and ten other people sitting there
talking to him, you got a table with eleven Nazis.
Unknown

"Fake friends are like four quarters.
They will change for a dollar."
Beanie Sigel

Tell me who you hang with,
and I'll tell you who you are
Unknown

They say, "blood is thicker than water" when it
comes to family or friends. I say, if we care, respect,
and love one another then love is thicker than blood
AND water.
Ignatius J

When you lose confidence in yourself, those who don't truly believe in
you lose confidence in you. Those who believe in you will help you find
your confidence.
Unknown

DON'T lie to anyone, unless you are comfortable
being lied to.
DON'T steal from anyone, unless you are prepared
to have something stolen from you.
DON'T cheat on anyone, unless you can handle
being cheated on.
What you do to others, others will eventually do the
same to you.
The moral of the story is . . .
"THE GOLDEN RULE"
Treat people how you want to be treated, even
when they don't treat you the way you want to
be treated. How they treat you is between THEM
and KARMA, not you
Ignatius J 25SEP14

Learn to deal with people for who they are,
not who you want them to be. Life gets a lot
easier when you stop expecting apple juice
from oranges
FACE THE REALITY
Unknown

I continuously sought out for solid
reliable friends in vain.
Disappointment after disappointment.
Expectations instead of acceptance
was my folly. I was alone then and I'm
alone now.
Teaching myself not to rely on others
for sincere genuine friendships is an
ongoing class for me. Learning to take
people at face value is easier said than
done, but it is a lesson that I have to
practice to master
Ignatius J 06JUN2022

"You can be with someone every day and still not
know who they really are until you are put in a situation
where hard decisions have to be made. Time doesn't
define where you stand in a person's life. Circumstances do."
Unknown

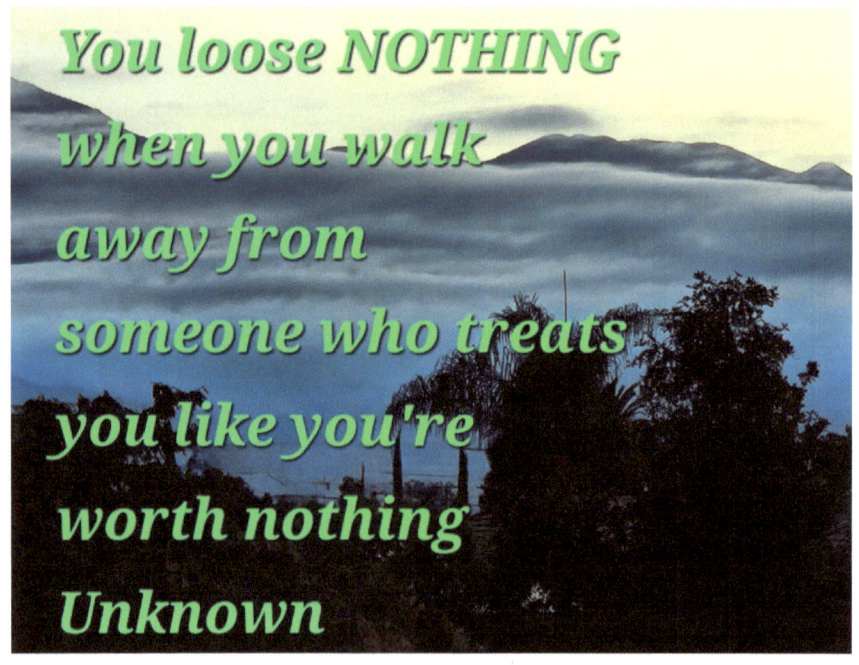

You loose NOTHING when you walk away from someone who treats you like you're worth nothing

Unknown

Photo by Ignatius J

"You can meet somebody tomorrow
who has better intentions for you than
someone you've known forever.
Time means almost nothing,
character does"
Unknown

"Him: If you show her that you care,
she will keep you as a spare . . .
(and leave your messages on read
for 12+ hours)
Her: That's just to show him he doesn't
supposed to be there; it's that we don't
care just know that we were AWARE"
Ronnell Art Tatum Bey & Kamela Bey

Hearts are wild creatures that's why
our ribs are cages.
Unknown

"The moment you
present a person with
ALL they want and they start
saying what they aren't ready
for: come to the conclusion
that they don't want it from
"YOU"."
Ignatius J

"Accept people as they are, but
place people where they belong."
Unknown

"This hit home for me!
When a flashlight grows dim or quits working,
you don't throw it away; you change the batteries.
When a person messes up
and finds themselves in a dark place,
do you cast them aside? Of course not,
you help them change their batteries!
Some need AA. Attention and affection,
Some need AAA... Attention, affection
and acceptance. Some need C...
Compassion. Some need D... Direction.
And if they still don't seem to shine.
simply sit with them quietly and
share your light."
Unknown

"There is no such thing as the unknown
just the temporary unhidden."
Captain James Tiberius kirk
Star Trek Beyond

"Healing makes you realize some people
don't deserve to be around you, no matter
how much you love them. Unconditional
love doesn't mean unconditional tolerance
of abuse, disrespect, or bullshit- it's not
unconditional boundaries."
Pammy DS- selflovehealer

"If you can't respect, honor, and
love yourself then there's nothing
you can do for me in a relationship."
Paul Hodges

They say you don't know what
you've got until it's gone, but
the truth is, you knew what
you had, you just thought you'd
never lose it
Unknown

"Surround yourself with humans who create their lives.
People who change, more than they complain. Create,
more than they consume. Live actively, instead of
accepting life as is. Find people chasing down their
potential."
@alpha_leaders

"When you feel like your presence in someone's life
is not appropriate, just remove yourself. This will save you
so much disappointment and the feelings of being an
after thought or last planned recovery. People will show love,
care, attention to whom they feel is important. Reclaiming
back our time is a vibe. The train has left the station."
Kwaku Ifadamilare

"Loving someone in addiction is like watching them
drown while refusing to grab the life raft. You can't
save them, but you can be there when they choose to
swim."
-Kayla

"Relationships are a corporation, and when we
run it like that, it builds. Selfish singular nature
will never grow anything."
Michael white

"God forbid someone have different beliefs
than you, and you wanna abuse them into yours."
Alana Anderson

Not everyone is qualified to know your house.
Some friendships should end in the office,
church, road and market
Unknown

DAMN, I really got some good ass memories
with people who can KISS MY WHOLE ASS!!
Unknown

"A wise person once told me,
"Let people do what they do, so you see what they'd do".
That'll answer all the questions you have."
Unknown

Energy is my first language.
I understand it more than I do
words. You might as well be who
you are because your vibe is
going to tell me the truth anyways.
Unknown

You lose NOTHING when you walk away from
someone who treats you like you're worth
NOTHING
Unknown

"Divorce is okay.

Breaking up is okay.

Starting over is okay.

Moving on is okay.

Saying "NO" is okay.

Being alone is okay.

What's not okay is staying in a relationship where you feel unhappy, unvalued, or unappreciated. Staying in that space only drains your spirit, dims your light, and robs you of the love and peace you truly deserve. Always choose yourself over settling for less than your worth."

Nico JA Jones

Photo by Ignatius J

Mindfulness

"Every single "problem" in your life is giving you
some type of information. When things are good,
no new information is being processed, but good
feelings are being experienced. But when things
get sticky, is when the information is pouring in.
Organize that info. Take a step back to get a better
view. Then get back at it. Keep going.
#everydaypower

"Maybe the journey isn't about
becoming anything.
Maybe it's about unbecoming
everything that isn't really you, so
that you can be who you were meant
to be in the 1st place."
Paulo Coelho

Photo by Ignatius J

I Was Dying

First, I was dying to finish high school and start college.

And then I was dying to finish college and start working.

And then I was dying to marry and have children.

And then I was dying for my children to grow old enough for school so I could return to work.

And then I was dying to retire.

And now, I am dying... and suddenly I realize I forgot to live.

Unknown

"We're directors of our life.

Every morning you call,

ACTION"

Ava DuVernay

The real glow up is when you stop waiting to

turn into some perfect version of yourself and

consciously enjoy being who you are in the present.

Unknown

"Just like how Instagram has its own algorithm
and shows you more of what you're interested in,
the entire universe also has an algorithm and
shows you more of what you are thinking, feeling,
and focusing on."
Charlamagne Tha God

"The highest form of knowledge is empathy,
for it requires us to suspend our egos and live
in another's world."
-Plato

"YOUR BODY: sight, touch, smell, taste, hear.
YOUR SOUL: mind, will, emotions, imagination, affection.
YOUR SPIRIT: prayer, praise, worship, faith, meditation."
mrgeoff13

You are holding a cup of coffee when someone comes along and bumps into you or shakes your arm, making you spill your coffee everywhere. Why did you spill the coffee?

"Because someone bumped into me!!!"

Wrong answer.

You spilled the coffee because there was coffee in your cup. Had there been tea in the cup, you would have spilled tea. Whatever is inside the cup is what will spill out. Therefore, when life comes along and shakes you (which WILL happen), whatever is inside you will come out. It's easy to fake it, until you get rattled. So, we have to ask ourselves "what's in my cup?"

When life gets tough, what spills over?

Joy, gratitude, peace, and humility?

Anger, bitterness, victim mentality, and quitting tendencies?

Life provides the cup; you choose how to fill it.

Today let's work towards filling our cups with gratitude, forgiveness, joy, words of affirmation, resilience, positivity; and kindness, gentleness, and love for others.

Unknown

The art of being wise is knowing who to ignore,
what to overlook, where to leave things, when to
move on and why is all necessary.
Unknown

"The only true wisdom is in knowing
you know nothing."
-Socrates

"When I run after what I think I want, my days are a furnace of stress
and anxiety; If I sit in my own place of patience, what I need flows to
me, without pain. From this I understand that what I want also wants
me, is looking for me and attracting me. There is a great secret here for
anyone who can grasp it."
-Rumi

Photo by Ignatius J

"Wait for happiness. I promise it exists. It might not feel like it right now, but one day you'll wake up and everything will just feel right. You'll be content with who you are and where you're going. Life will just make sense. You'll still have good days and bad days, but it's okay because you'll know everything is as it should be"

Charlotte Freeman/ Power of Wordz

"I'll never regret the love I gave anyone, even if it wasn't reciprocated, love always comes back full circle, that love is coming back to me in some shape or form. Keep putting love into the universe, cause it's coming back with interest."

-BOII MCCOY

I hope this time when you see the signs, you don't ignore them. I hope this time when you see the lack of effort, you don't force it. You pick up and go. I hope this time you save yourself before you even get damaged.

Unknown

I can literally manifest anything.
If I want it, I will get it. That's my
belief and I stand firm in it.

Unknown

De ja vu is a marker in time left by your higher self. This is to wake you from your slumber. You have but one life. You're in control. Take note, is this the life you want. It brings you instantly into the present. To analyze your life.

Unknown

Worrying is like worshipping the problem.
Prayer is surrendering your problem.
You give it energy, validity, and motion.
Give your energy to what you want more of
in your life.

Unknown

If you worry, don't' pray.
If you pray, don't worry.

Unknown

"The opposite of aging is death.
Not getting a birthday means you
die. Your greatest gift from God is
a birthday."

Kendra G

"When I look back on my life,
I see pain, mistakes, and heartache.
When I look in the mirror, I see strength,
learned lessons, and pride in myself"
Heartfeltquotes. Blogspot.com

Ain't nothing to it but to do it. If you don't use it OR abuse
it you'll lose it. No time for prolonged procrastination.
No time for prolonged hesitation. Movement comes from
motivation. What you do day in, and day out is your
creation that derives from your dedication. Keep going.
Ignatius J 09SEP2024

"The only true wisdom is in knowing you know nothing."
-Socrates

Photo by Ignatius J

"I seen a rainbow yesterday

But too many storms have come and gone

Leavin' a trace of not on God-given ray

Is it because my life is ten shades of gray

I pray all ten fade away

Seldom praise Him for the sunny days

And like his promise is true

Only my faith can undo

The many chances I blew

Will it bring my life to anew

Clear blue and unconditional skies

Have dried the tears from my eyes

No more lonely cries

My only bleedin' hope is for the folk who can't cope

Wit' such an endurin' pain

That it keeps 'em in the pourin rain

Who's to blame for tootin' cane in your vein

What a shame

You shoot and aim for someone else's brain

You calm the insane and name this day in time

For fallin' prey to crime

I say the system got you victim to your own mind

Dreams are hopeless aspirations

In hopes of comin' true

Believe in yourself

The rest is up to me and you

Don't go chasing waterfalls

Please stick to the rivers and the lakes that you're used to

I know you're gonna have it your way or nothing at all
But I think you're moving too fast
Marqueze/ Lisa Lopes/ Organized Noize

Lovin Me

"Stop letting people put you in the "just in case" pile. The back up pile. The last resort section. Because people will walk away from you, go explore other options, and once they realize the grass isn't greener, here they come, wanting to pick you up again. And some of you take that as a compliment. It's not. If someone isn't choosing you consistently, choose yourself. You deserve better than to be somebody's backup plan just in case what they think is better doesn't work out. Shut the revolving door and honor your boundaries. You deserve more."

David Byant Smith Jr.

Love doesn't fix us. And it's not supposed to. Love is a motivator. Love should inspire us to do better. To be better. But humans are creatures of habit. And even in the best situations. Breaking habits takes time. It takes effort. It takes commitment to growth. And all the love in the world won't make someone grow who is dead set on remaining the same.

Unknown

"I want you to begin again. I want you to let your hurts heal and let the past be just that, the past. I want you to open yourself up and embrace the present moment. I want you to stand in your faith and watch your fears fade away. Yes, I want you to begin again."

-Dale Evans

You will be happy again, you will be more yourself than ever, you will understand your heart better when you heal, you will be okay.

Unknown

Make sure your glow up happens on the inside first. Let your mental, emotional, and spiritual health reach the highest of levels. Let your physical health be a beautiful reflection of what your soul looks like on the inside. Great things are happening for you. Great things are being prepared for you. Great things are destined to appear on your journey. Your intuition already knows this; its time your mind and heart catch up. Raise your head high and raise your faith even higher. Embrace the exciting road leading up to your dreams; they're already taken care of.

Unknown

"You're going to meet some people who are intimidated by you. You're different. People don't know how to react or how to accept people who don't follow the crowd . . . They are not used to someone who doesn't fit in- so instead of bolstering your uniqueness, they'll try to make you feel like you're weird or damaged. I'm here to offer some well- earned advice: SCREW THEM" -

Alfa (Alfawrites) You're Different

"We have to work on our boundaries.
We can't be everything to everyone
and nothing to ourselves."
Shana Bueford- Wilder

"What doesn't kill you can:

* Dysregulate your nervous system

* Trap itself in your body

* Steal your sense of self

* Make you wish it did

I don't know what "makes you stronger"

means but let's stop glorifying trauma as

a life- lesson we've been blessed with."

Dr. Jen (Neuropsychologist)

""Your trauma made you stronger."

No, my trauma made me traumatized, it made me weak, gave me
sleepless nights, and memory loss, it gave me feelings I've never wanted.
I made myself stronger, by dragging myself out of a dark place and
dealing with the consequences that weren't my fault."

-RK @rkkaaayou

"And then I realized that I can choose to be excited

over my future rather than be torn up over my past."

J. Strelou

"And then I realized that I can choose to be excited over my future rather than be torn up over my past." J. Strelou

Photo by Ignatius J

"Procrastination is not the absence of will- it's the presence of pain, a quiet signal of a battle fought in silence. It's not laziness; It's the weight of an invisible storm pressing on the soul, a resistance born not from boredom but from unspoken wounds.

We procrastinate not because we don't care but because we care so deeply that it immobilizes us. Each delayed task whispers a fear of failure, perfectionism masked as avoidance, or the simple exhaustion of a spirit too weary to carry the load. Procrastination is the hearts way of pausing, asking, "Are you sure we're ready for this?"

But here's the breathtaking truth: it transforms once you meet it with understanding instead of judgment. Like a river unblocked, the energy that procrastination held captive begins to flow. It reveals that the time you thought you were wasting was time spent holding space for your own healing.

And then, almost like magic, it dissolves- not through force, but through love. You awaken to the realization that time was never your enemy. You forget how to waste it because every moment, even the quiet ones, becomes sacred. Procrastination isn't a flaw. It's a map leading you back to the places within yourself that ache for your kindness, courage, and light. Listen to it. Heal through it. And when you emerge on the other side, you'll find a version of yourself you never knew you were becoming- a self-unburdened, unstoppable, free."

Katie Kamara

Loss

"A grieving person is going to laugh
again, and smile again . . . They're
going to move forward. But that doesn't
mean that they've moved on."
Nora Mcinerny

"We were taught to get the best and highest degrees.
Shoot for the stars. Forge a new path. Be bold. Don't
back down. Then the evil murderer called premature
death comes and takes you. Some say it was your destiny.
I say sometimes evil wins. That is the reality. No matter how
temporary the win may be."
Cleo Gordon

"Every old man that dies is a library that burns"
Amadou Hampate Ba

"Death is NOT the opposite of life, but a part of it."
Haruki Murakami

"To live in the hearts we leave behind is not to die."
-*Thomas Campbell*

"The life of the dead is placed in the memory of the living."
Marcus Tullius Cicero

To a well-organized mind, death is but the next great adventure."
Albus Dumbledore

"Death is nature's way of saying, 'Your table is ready.'"
Robin Williams

"No one is actually dead until the ripples they
cause in the world die away."
Terry Pratchett

"As a caterpillar becomes a butterfly,
so the spirit is transformed."
Unknown

Photo by Ignatius J

Death leaves a heartache no one can heal,
love leaves a memory no one can steal.
Unknown

"The fear of death follows from the fear of life.
A man who lives fully is prepared to die at any time."
Mark Twain

"Although it's difficult today to see beyond the sorrow, may looking
back in memory help comfort you tomorrow."
Unknown

"The risk of love is loss, and the price of loss is grief –But the
pain of grief is only a shadow when compared with the pain of
never risking love."
Hillary Stanton Zunin

"Grief is not a disorder, a disease or a sign of weakness. It is an
emotional, physical and spiritual necessity, the price you pay for love.
The only cure for grief is to grieve."
Earl Grollman

Tracy died after a long fought civil war
Just after I'd wipe away his last tear
I guess he's better off than he was before
A whole lot better off than the fool's he left here
I used to cry for Tracy because he was my only
friend
Those kind of cars don't pass you every day
I used to cry for Tracy because I wanted to see
him again
But sometimes, sometimes life ain't always the
way
Springtime was always my favorite time of year
A time for lovers holding hands in the rain
Now springtime only reminds me of Tracy's
tears
Always cry for love, never cry for pain
I often dream of heaven, and I know Tracy's
there
I know that he has found another friend
Maybe one day I'll see Tracy again
Sometimes it snows in April, sometimes I feel so
bad
Sometimes I wish that life was never ending
But all good things, they say never last
And love, isn't love until it's passed
Prince Rogers Nelson, Lisa Coleman/
Wendy Melvoin

"The little boy with the dark brown eyes didn't realize how deep his dark brown eyes were. The little boy with the deep dark brown eyes didn't know how rich his ebony skin was. The little boy with the deep dark brown eyes, and rich ebony skin didn't understand his beautiful jet- black wooly hair. The little boy with the deep dark brown eyes, rich ebony skin, and beautiful jet-black wooly hair didnt grasp his astonishingly exquisite full lips. The little boy with the deep dark brown eyes, rich ebony skin, beautiful jet-black wooly hair, and astonishingly exquisite full lips couldn't see how remarkable his flawless-aligned ivory teeth shined. The little boy with the deep dark brown eyes, rich ebony skin, beautiful jet-black wooly hair, astonishingly exquisite full lips, and flawless aligned ivory teeth had no idea of how magnificently perfect he is, until I told him, " You are. I know because I am you".
Ignatius J 06JAN2025

Other books in the works:

- The Second Baby Mama –Now What's Next??

Coming Soon:

- Don't Be Meme
- Ignatius J -The Attendant

Published Books:

- Two Baby Mamas, an Ex-Wife, and an Ex-Boyfriend – Now What's Next??
- Ignatius J P's & Q's and Words of Inspiration VOL I
- The Ex-Wife –Now What's' Next??

www.ingramcontent.com/pod-product-compliance
Lightning Source LLC
Chambersburg PA
CBHW040855120626
46551CB00001B/28